LEARN Funk Guitar
WITH TOWER OF POWER'S
JEFF TAMELIER

CONTENTS

Thanks to Fender USA and Europe, Jim Dunlop, Inc., and Associates, Dean Markley Strings, Line 6, Seymour Duncan, Brad Townsend, Michelle Zarin, Guitar Center (Concord, CA), Jack Forchette, Rhonda Espy, Randy Michaels, Tower of Power, and all our fans.

To John Stix (it's always nice to make a new friend in this business anytime and anywhere), Mark Pleis (Blind Gym), my fantastic family, Jesse, Justin, and Samantha, and to the greatest partner on the planet, my wife, Debi.

A special thanks to our great rhythm section. Every night it is truly an honor and a pleasure. To all other rhythm sections, remember, there is strength in numbers. PLAY TOGETHER!!!!

Transcribed by Jeff Jacobson

ISBN 1-57560-612-7

Visit our website at www.cherrylane.com

Foundations of Funky Rhythm Guitar

by Jeff Tamelier

In preparing to write this book I did some research on the roots of soul music and how the guitar fit in. We start with the banjo. During the slavery era this was the first real instrument that was strummed. They called it a *bonjour*. Heading up to New Orleans, that's where the banjo fit in with Dixieland, and that form of comping got mainstreamed. The guitar was originally used primarily as an acoustic instrument with the big bands. Rhythm guitar was very much the glue between the bass and the drums. The drummer and bass player are kind of going off and the musical glue is the rhythm guitar. Freddie Green in the Count Basie Band was fabulous at this technique. The guy had such a nice low mid fat thing going on, he almost sounded like another drum. I remember Ray Charles' *Genius + Soul = Jazz* record, which had Freddie Green with Quincy Jones arrangements. Then on the pop side, if you listen to the Platters, the rhythm guitar is way in the background. It's almost used as a quarter note kind of comp thing.

Sun Records was very important too. Scotty Moore with Elvis was a little out of the norm. It was half lead, half rhythm, but definitely comping. Those periods were very important. But James Brown had the first real funky hypnotic rhythm guitar thing that I was hip to. In his early days he used Les Buie, but his most famous guitarist was Jimmy "Scratch" Nolen. He also used Alphonso "Country" Kellum and Catfish Phelps. But it's Jimmy Nolen playing on "Papa's Got a Brand New Bag" and "Payback." He is the cream of the crop. A lot of times Nolen would play with "Country" Kellum. Sometimes he wouldn't even sound a chord—he would just do scratch for one chord. They'd work beautifully together. It was more percussive. There was Pig Jacobs from Dyke and the Blazers, who were originally from Buffalo, and they came out to Phoenix. He was the writer of "Funky Broadway" long before we knew it from Wilson Pickett. They were pretty obscure but they had a lot of 9th chords. Freddie Stone and Sly [Stone] really brought it to arena rock. Curtis Mayfield was my favorite R&B ballad guitarist.

One good way to look at various rhythm guitar styles is to explore it by region. There was New Orleans with Leo Nocentelli from the Meters. He is killer. Check out "Look-Ka Py Py," one of their first records. The Meters are kind of the New Orleans version of Booker T. & the MG's, playing basically instrumental tunes. That's a great record to hear Leo and a rhythm section really playing together. He has a real bite to his playing. They played on a lot of the Dr. John stuff; "Right Place Wrong Time" is the Meters. I believe towards the end of his career, Fats Domino used the Meters. Same with Lee Dorsey, who used the Meters on "Working in a Coal Mine." The Meters were coming up young and those guys were older, so they learned from the best.

The Philly sound was Bobby Eli and Norman Harris. Listen to all the Thom Bell and Gamble & Huff–produced records, the Stylistics, the Spinners, the Delfonics, the wave of stuff from the '70s. The Philly Sigma sound can be heard on David Bowie's "Fame." That's all Philly players, as is any old Spinners tune, like "I'll Be Around." There are great guitar parts on that song.

You have Steve Cropper with Booker T. and the Memphis sound. Memphis is Cropper all the way, and afterwards Bobby Womack slides in there. For Cropper, listen to one of my favorites: "Ninety-Nine and a Half (Won't Do)," by Wilson Pickett. You've got "Soul Man" and "Knock on Wood." That band took a lot of hard left turns in their bridges. They would go from A to D to E, and then to A-flat on the bridge. Check out early Wilson Picket, Rufus Thomas's "Walkin' the Dog," or Otis Redding.

In Detroit you had the Funk Brothers from Motown. They used three guys working as a team. One guy was playing the backbeats, one guy was playing all the fills, and one guy was on the chords. Sometimes they would play the same chord in different parts—overtones and harmonic patterns. "I Want You Back" by The Jackson 5 is two killer guitar parts. Listen to "My Cherie Amour," "It's a Shame," and "I'm Gonna Make You Love Me." It's all there. Another thing I think of is that one tone on "The Way You Do the Things You Do." I later learned that sound was all done on Gibsons. It was done with big fat L-5's, a Super 400, and an ES-175 with the treble pickup and flatwound strings. It's so Fender sounding. Freddie Stone and Johnny "Guitar" Watson could also make a Gibson sound like a Fender. I dug what those guys did with tones and their parts.

On the West Coast you've got Freddie Stone with "Thank You (Falettinme Be Mice Elf Agin)" and "You Can Make It If You Try." I put the East Bay sound, Sly & the Family Stone, and Tower of Power together. And in L.A. you had Charles Wright and the Watts 103rd Street Rhythm Band, with pre–Earth, Wind & Fire's Al McKay and "Express Yourself." I also dig Tony Maiden from Rufus and Paul Jackson, Jr., who played on countless session recordings in the '80s.

There's Muscle Shoals, Alabama, with Jimmy Johnson. You've got this region in the south and soul music was right there. "Clean Up Woman" with Little Beaver in Florida. James Brown in Georgia with "Lickin' Stick," and "I Got the Feeling." "Papa's Got a Brand New Bag" is the one everybody goes to.

The East Coast had all those great Atlantic records on which Cornell Dupree played brilliant rhythm guitar. The Aretha Franklin and Donny Hathaway records are still some of my favorites.

Curtis Mayfield was in Chicago with the Impressions. They had "It's Alright," "Gypsy Woman," and "I'm So Proud." Curtis took pretty chords and made them real soulful.

Jeff Tamelier on Funk Guitar: An Interview

by John Stix

How do you take a chord progression that rocks with barre chords and make it into funk rhythm guitar?

The rock attack has more of its teeth in it. Funk rhythm needs to be more in the fabric of everything else. There's got to be more air in it. Playing with a drummer like Tower of Power's Dave Garibaldi, you learn how to do that. He does a lot of *ghosting*—real light notes, called *ghost notes*. Rocco Prestia, Tower's bassist, does them too. They are not notes. They are percussive type things. There are times when I need to leave air ("What Is Hip" 0:23-0:40). There are also times I need to scratch through it. Sometimes you need to lay out, maybe play a little lighter and let other bits kind of bubble up. That's a big part of the sound of our band. Funk music is definitely section oriented. If you listen to all those rhythm sections I mentioned, you can hear what everyone is doing, and there is a purpose to everything they do. You put it together and the strength goes right through it. I think the guitar is the driving force that makes you bob your head. But you've got to play in the fabric of the music.

Whereas with rock music you want to play aggressively. I played with the Starship for five years, so I've done that too. I had two Marshall stacks and did all the solos. It was a wider sound. With a funk rhythm section it's more like being in the studio—you want the bass here, the guitar here, and the organ over there. The section is just one thing and you can see the threads of the fabric. The guitar is more tucked. You hear everything else; you feel everything else.

A lot of times I use fewer notes in my chords, so maybe my bass notes won't ring out. There are a lot of two-note or three-note fingerings. There is a little spot for them. It cuts a little better. Maybe the keyboard is playing on a higher register so I'll do something a little lower, because there is sonically more of a spot for me there.

I use a lot of tritones. The 3rd and 7th of a dominant 7th chord is an example of a tritone. If I were playing an E7 chord, for example, I would play G-sharp and D. You can move that tritone shape up and down the neck. It's cool because there is no root and no 5th. As you move down the neck fret by fret, if you think of the missing—but implied—roots as going through a cycle of 5ths, the functions of the notes of the tritone flip-flop as you move down: 3–7, then 7–3, then 3–7, and so on. It's called a tritone because the interval is the distance of three whole steps. I use that quite a bit, or maybe add a 9th for the fourth hit rather than just always pound on the 9th. (See Ex. 1.)

TRACK 01

Ex. 1: Tritone with 9th

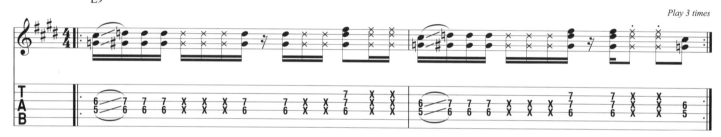

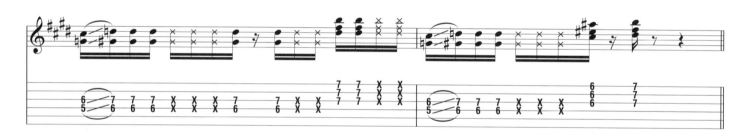

You feel your spots. That's very important in funk guitar. If you give yourself too much, you're not sitting right either sonically or volume-wise. Sonically it's very important to hear yourself in the band. We can use the word *fabric* throughout this whole book and that's what it is, playing with huge ears ("F-Funk" 0:12-0:41).

Not many people start off by wanting to play two-note chords in the fabric of the sound.

It took years of being in bands. I've been in horn bands since I was 14, playing TOP and Sly's music. It's stuff you learn from older guys who have been there. Maybe you're sticking out a little there. It's a process of elimination. When you're young, you're so eager to get out there and play. One thing I've always done with any type of music I've heard is I've gone a couple of chapters back from the guys I'm studying to find out where they learned their stuff from. It gives me a clearer vision of what they were thinking about. Obviously what they were thinking about is kind of what I'm thinking about because I learned from them. Jeff Beck is my favorite, even though he is not considered funk. He is my God. Who could he have listened to? It was Cliff Gallup—the guy from Gene Vincent. That was his guy. So I'd go back and start buying Gene Vincent records and go, Wow man, this guy is off the hook!

Who do you listen to on stage during a Tower performance?

I'm listening to everybody. Rocco and Dave together are one of the great rhythm sections. I think it's because Rocco's style is so unorthodox. The way he learned to play, his whole concept, the whole way he comes to music, is very different. He couldn't tell you who played on what. He goes by sounds. He gave me this great example. When he and Dave first started playing together, Dave would be on his hi-hat and Rocco would play real short. Dave would go to his bell and Rocco would play longer notes. Dave would say, "I noticed when I went to my bell you played bigger notes?" Rocco goes, "Well, it's a bigger sound. The cymbal is a wider sound." That has nothing to do with anything you write down or learn or listen to, it's just pure instinctive musicianship. Rocco does that more then anyone else in the band. I'm right next to him. I play to Dave's time, but as far as the feel of the band, it's Rocco. His outlook is real unusual…the short notes…it's a little on top. TOP music is a little more on top of the beat and the Meters may be behind. We're more on the tip of our toes all the time. I'm sonically a glue where there needs to be some sort of chording happening, still with 16th notes in mind. That's how I count—16th notes. When the horns come in and do their hits, I'm there already because I'm thinking like that. A lot of guys go "1 and 2 and 3 and 4." There are 16th notes in between those eighth notes that you are kind of guessing if you're really not feeling it that way. Or even quarter notes. There are three more notes in there that are going to be accounted for, and you're not always going to be right there unless you are all counting the same. We all have to be on the same page as to where it's felt, and with Tower it's 16th notes on top of the beat.

Is your right hand doing the 16ths anyway, and you hit when you want to hit?

Sometimes there are songs where scratching [strumming muted strings] kind of covers up the ghosting. A good example for that is Tower's first guitar player Willie Fulton. He was more of a scratcher. Bruce Conte [followed Willie in TOP] played more in the holes. He didn't scratch as much, because he had a keyboard player to play with. Chester Thompson joined the band when Bruce joined the band. Willie was a three-piece. He needed to play a little more open. There was a little more stuff for him to fill.

What can you tell guitarists about getting their rhythm together? Rhythm is hard to get; you have to feel it.

It's more of a self-taught type of thing. It's definitely a feel. Get a metronome and put it on 16th notes or eighth notes or whatever the song is you're working on. If it's "Ninety-Nine and a Half," that's more of an eighth-note thing. If you can master the 16th-note rhythm, which is a lot of the James Brown stuff, the other stuff is a little easier to understand. It's easier to put in the pocket. There's less stuff.

Is there a "walk before you can run" aspect to playing funk guitar? With single notes you can do scales.

I like to do this going back almost to Elvis and that quarter note style. Then the Beatles were a little more lively, and then there's Sly Stone with the 16th notes wah part in "Thank You." It's basically the same lick felt three different ways. It's very important that whatever the tune is, find out where everyone else is feeling it. If the drummer is feeling 16th notes and I'm feeling eighth notes, there are going to be flams going on. (See Exs. 2, 3, and 4.)

TRACK 02

Ex. 2: à la Elvis

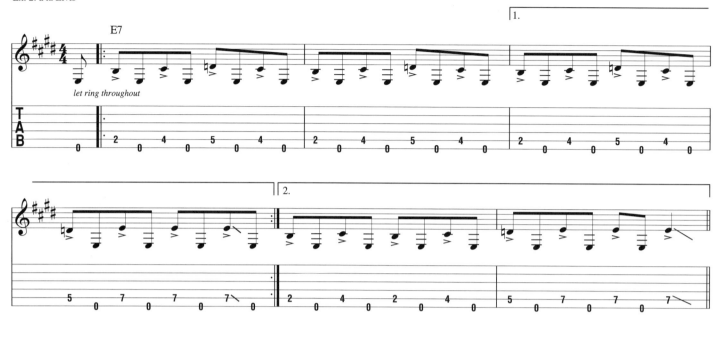

TRACK 03

Ex. 3: à la Chuck Berry/Beatles

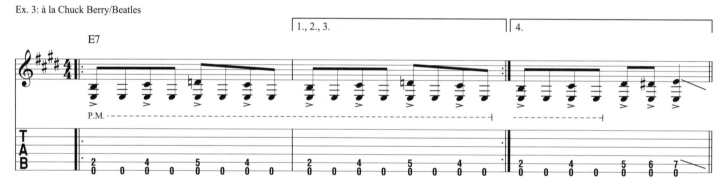

TRACK 04

Ex. 4: à la Sly Stone

Has funk rhythm guitar evolved since the '60s and '70s?

I think it's de-volved. It's decreased a little bit. There is so much more emphasis on other things in R&B music. It's more about a great track and a great loop. They will have a guy come in and play a couple of bars and place it in there.

What about the importance of the wah pedal?

People are so into sounds and samples these days, they think of it more as a good sample sound. Freddie Stone is the wah-wah king. There are guys who came along later who got more credit for it and maybe even used it in their name, but to me Freddie Stone was doing that stuff in the mid-'60s. Listen to "Thank You (Falettinme Be Mice Elf Agin)." There is one guitar that starts on the last 16th note of beat 1 which he did a lot. It was kind of his thing. The wah on that song ("Free Fallin Funk" 0:02-0:42) was more on the downbeat.

Tell me about the use of octaves.

The master of octaves on guitar would be Wes Montgomery. For funk, I think once again it was Sly with Freddie Stone. That octave thing is a very good glue. I like to use octaves when chords are changing, and I'll stay on the same note. It's kind of like a string part where you let the chords do the movement. On "Credit" I'm doing an F octave against a Dm, F/C, A♭/B♭—those three chords (0:44-0:53). Playing with Tower I can voice stuff that fits better with the horns. An octave is a simple approach that works very well. (See Ex. 5.)

TRACK 05

Ex. 5: Octave Rhythm

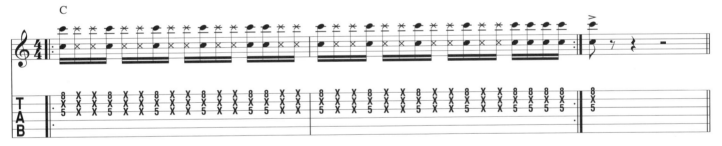

The Philly thing has a lot of octaves in it, as on "I'll Be Around." (See Ex. 6.)

TRACK 06

Ex. 6: à la Philly Octave Pattern

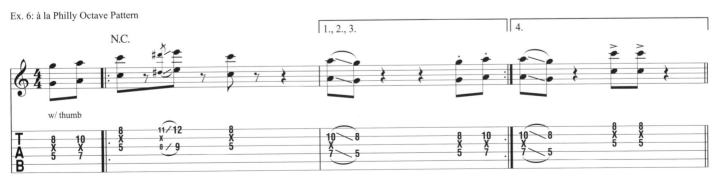

Kind of a jazz-funk crossover. There is a lot of jazz influence in funk, mainly because of the off-beats and off rhythms. I've read it has a lot to do with the Latins heading up to Spainish Harlem and hitting the Cotton Club and taking the straight swing and adding the clave rhythm. I think a lot of funk came out of that.

Let's explore the playing on the eight songs. Tell us about "Hip-E-Jam."

It's sort of a Freddie Stone thing. It starts as a two-note wah pedal thing. Effects came into play a lot with funk guitar in the '70s with Parliament. I'm using two different effects on there. I have a flanger and a wah on there for an unusual sound. It's more of a low two-note thing I'm doing in the first part. Since we're in E, I can always let the E string ring (0:03-0:35). I can go all the way up the neck just using the 6th and 5th strings. (See Ex. 7.)

TRACK 07

Ex. 7: Two-String (5th & 6th) Wah Pattern

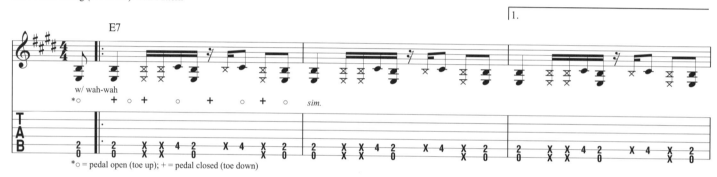

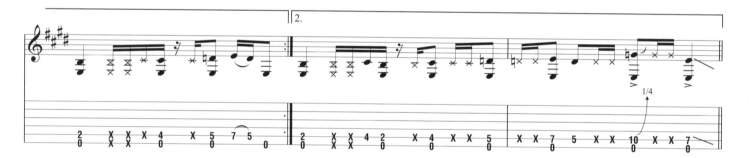

There is one other thing I do here: a pull-off I learned from listening to Sly. I slide up from the 5th fret to the 6th, then I go the 4th and pull off to the 3rd. It's unusual; I've never heard anyone do it but Sly and the Family Stone. You get the 16th-note feel to it.

Remember to hit beat 1 hard. There is air in this part. I use my thumb on this one too. So we are using the tonic E note on one string, and always having it going. With the other string I come up with a little melodic counter melody that's low, but it's still a rhythm part. You can make the chord minor or major, or even sus4. (See Ex. 8.)

TRACK 08

Ex. 8: Two-String (5th & 6th) Wah Pattern w/ Sus4

Can you play different parts in the start of this song?

Absolutely. As long as you get the low E ringing, you can play around with the 6th and 7th—as long as you have the 16th notes and the downbeat on "1." You really lay into it rather than wait for it. (See Ex. 9.)

TRACK 09

Ex. 9: Two-String (5th & 6th) Pattern Using the 6th & 7th

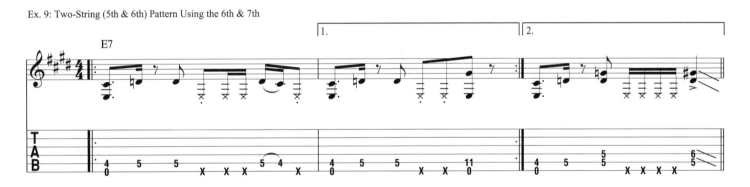

At the beginning, the guitar is playing on beat 1, and at 0:37 Roger [Smith, keyboard player for TOP] and I swap. I let Roger play on beat 1, and I leave a big space there, which is the opposite of the opening. He is hitting this kind of lush New York rooftop jazz type of chord, and he needs to be there. There is none of the 16th note scratching because the chord on beat 1 is lush. I need to give him space to play it. Otherwise, it would take away from this completely cool thing he is doing. If you notice, when we swap parts I wait another eight or 16 bars and then I start adding little chord hits, basically dominant 7th type of chords. It's a two-bar phrase.

Talk to me about upstrokes versus downstrokes?

I use upstrokes when I'm syncopating with the snare or the rest of the band. Upstrokes seem shorter. You hear the high short notes first. A lot of times I play the 9th chords with just the three strings for that exact reason. I think they are very important for syncopation. (See Ex. 10.)

Ex. 10: Three-String 9th Chord

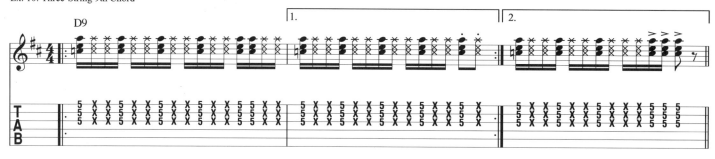

"Don't Knock It"

You'll notice in the beginning I'm not playing. There is another rule that sometimes the best thing to play in funk guitar is nothing at all. This is more of an organ solo. What I'm trying to do is let him dictate how he's feeling at the time. It changes nightly. I let the three of them get into a thing. I want to make what I'm doing behind him so comfortable that he can just go off and it still feels like he's kind of comping. I do eight bars of D9, so I have a partial line and on that I add a 5th. That's why I talk about playing two notes, maybe three notes. Off that I don't even have to move. I'm adding notes so it makes it sound like I'm moving (0:33-0:45). I've got the 16th note thing happening in the right hand. Once again it's the ears; I let the organ dictate where he is feeling the thing. It is his solo.

The lesson here is the addition of the notes?

Let's play a tritone. You have your 3/7 here on D7. For G7 you go down one fret and you have 7/3. My movement is subtle, real close, real tight. (See Ex. 11.)

Ex. 11: Tritone, D7–G7

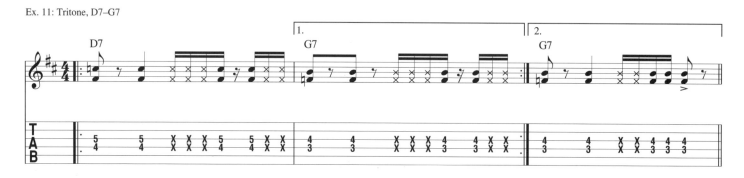

Every 16 bars I kind of change gears. I was down here on the 4th fret and I moved up to D minor at the 10th fret. That's going to make me try different stuff. I have a G9 here, which I couldn't do down the neck. Since I switch to minor I go into this 4ths thing that I like. (See Ex. 12.)

Ex. 12: 4ths Pattern on Am7

You hear that a lot. Check out Bruce Conte, Tower's second guitar player. It's like Herbie Hancock with his left hand. I play 4ths in this song. The lesson is to try different positions. If you're changing gears and going up, sometimes you can make gear changes with sound, and maybe with a higher chord. If everybody is playing a little harder, a higher chord might cut through a little better.

"Down to the Nightclub"

The Verse on this is kind of my homage to TOP's first two guitar players. Willie Fulton recorded this song originally. He didn't play with a keyboard player so his thing was more a full Bb7 chord. When they did the *Live and in Living Color* record they had Chester Thompson on keyboards. Bruce's part was totally different. I kind of do both, 'cause I think they are both cool (0:15-0:32). I get the full chords in there and it's so Cropper. The sliding part is very cool too. The lesson would be switching from a big chord to maybe a two-note thing. I'm taking charge in the first part. I'm kind of in the forefront. Then in the middle I have a little tucked part (0:24-0:32). It's a "picking your spots" kind of thing. I think I use my thumb too.

"Credit"

"Credit" is kind of whacked because the Verse is really behind the beat (0:04-0:16). You wait for the "1." When we go to the Verse, we're on top of the beat on 16ths (0:30-0:37). It's almost a 2 feel.

Funk guitar is its own thing as far as the chords. If you play an F major, I'll play an F minor every once in a while; it really doesn't matter. (See Ex. 13.)

Ex. 13: Playing F7 or Fm7

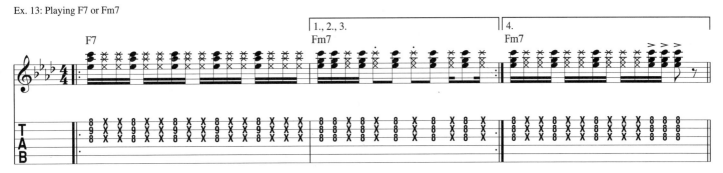

But if you were doing a jazz chart they would say, "That's got to be a 7th or that's got to be a minor." That's not the point; the point is the right hand and the glue. That's what's really important. The lesson is two different kinds of feels. In the Chorus I'm playing kind of behind, and I'm back on top for the Verses.

Tell me about muting.

There's the scratch, which is a form of muting. To do this, a lot of guys will mute the strings with their left hand and then strum with the right, producing a percussive sound. I use two different kinds of muting. I use my right hand palm to make things short. I strum and palm-mute at the same time. The other way is to use the left hand and barely take the fingers off. For this I'd use that more on an upstroke. Listen to James Brown's guys, Jimmy Nolen and "Country" Kellum, or Freddie Stone and Steve Cropper. Cropper was the master of going from A to D. He is doing more picking off the strings. It makes it short and more percussive. Funk guitar is very much percussion oriented.

"Free Falling Funk"

Dm6 is the basis of this Tower rhythm section groove we came up with. It's very James Brown oriented. I am locked into a part. I'm trying to do two James Brown guitar players at once, even though I overdubbed a wah part. It's got the minor 6 which is the "Big Payback" chord by James Brown. I'm doing it here as a Dm6. It does sound like a 13 if you have good ears. It's a two-bar phrase that is my own thing (0:00-0:33). Remember how I said the minor and the major don't really matter when you're playing funk? This gives you more weapons. I'm playing a single note 7–6–7, and this chord will actually be a D13#9. It's real short and leaves a little hole for that line. The lesson is the combination of trying to do two James Brown guitar parts at once. They used to call it heaven and hell. One guy would be strumming and one guy would be picking. I'm trying to do two parts at once and still feel the 16ths. There are little spots for me, and one time I do a single line (0:04-0:07) and the next I fill with a short chord (0:08-0:09). You have the chords, you have a little line, you leave a little air.

I'm feeling 16ths but I'm not playing them all. A lot of guys have to play all the 16ths to feel the 16ths. It's funkier if you don't. The whole thing that makes stuff funky is if you land on the upbeat. If everybody did it, it would be a big goulash of whatever. I often play on the second 16th of the beat. Scratching through the whole thing and then leaving out a few hits is a good way to practice. You'll feel the difference. You'll hear it obviously, but the feel is also different. You fill in your little spots with the drums because you are thinking 16th notes.

"F- Funk"

This song contains many of the same techniques we've talked about in other songs. This organ solo I approach differently. I start it out for Roger to follow me. I'm doing what we did earlier. I'm starting on two notes, maybe adding a third or fourth note here and there. I'll come down low (1:01-1:10), plays 4ths (1:55-2:00), tritones, two-, three-, and four-note chords (0:12-0:20), kind of mixing them up in a two-bar pattern. The idea is to come up with a part that's hypnotic but not distracting. If you lay into a part that is hypnotic and really funky, then people don't listen to you—they feel you. I'm in F so there is no open E. I go back to my Chuck Berry, but play it like Sly.

You can make up your own parts for this song?

It's a little more open. It's more of a jam. I was more experimental, I could wear more hats. We're more locked in to a part for the whole tune and maybe on the fourth bar everybody goes off. Until then it's pretty much the same thing. At the end of the fourth or eighth bar, if you want to do a rhythm fill at the end of the phrase, it's nice to do that (2:32-2:37). That's usually when the drums play a fill. I am thinking about what Dave might do here. I have the 16th notes in mind. Usually the end of the phrase is a good place to put something else in to push into the next section. We know Dave is going to go to the bell, so we are all going to change gears.

"Only So Much Oil in the Ground"

I think of this song as a big band funk arrangement and of myself as an ensemble player in a big band. The horns are prominent. I play this tune a lot like Bruce Conte recorded it. I add a few things of my own. It's ensemble funk guitar where you try to stay invisible. This is a fabric part. There are parts where I am syncopating with the snare (0:00-0:30). I call this center field guitar. All the things we've been talking about, I'm doing them all. I am playing within the fabric of the band even more so. I'm playing big chords because the organ is filling a lot. I sonically need to take up more room. A lesson in this one would be a wider approach to guitar, big chords, a heavy downbeat on "1," syncopation. There's a lot of big and short that we've talked about. This has both. On the word "only" I play big. I am kind of mirroring everything that goes on (0:48-1:05). Having huge ears on this tune is very important. There is syncopation going on with the drums. Bigger chords are going on because there are a lot of keyboard fills. I'm doing a lot of hits with the horns where I alter chords to have the right one to fit with the chord. Sometimes I play a minor 11 against their minor 7 and it sounds really cool. At the end of the Chorus when they sing "There is only so much oil," I emphasize the "2" rather then the "1." The lesson for this is ensemble big band funk guitar.

Did Bruce Conte write his own guitar part for this song?

Yes. The way I write my parts, they come in with a sketch and let us do what we want. Emillio [Castillo] is very good with guitar parts. I'm lucky. Ninety percent of what I come up with we keep. But he'll say, "Why don't you put this in here?" He is really dialed into guitar. It's cool to have a producer who is like that.

"What Is Hip"

I remember I was 13 when I first heard this. This tune improved TOP's vertical leap quite a bit. This is a perfect example of not hitting all the 16th ghost notes. This is the ghost note national anthem for funk. It's a great example of playing the hits where they are supposed to be. There is no in between stuff. I stay out of the way of the ghost 16th notes on the bass and drums (0:22-0:42). The lesson here is playing your parts where they land, at least on the Verses. I also added my own invention there. It's a two-string lick. I'm taking the root and 3rd and going up from D to E. I mirror the bass. It's kind of my own part. It's not too loud (0:42-0:50).

Give me a glossary of common funk chord voicings, a Funk Chord Dictionary.

Everybody knows this is a simple D chord:

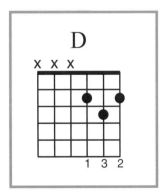

But it's also a Gmaj9:

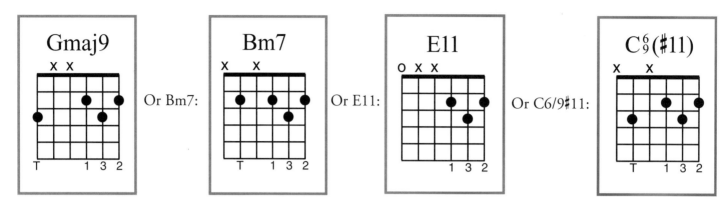

It's a bunch of things. A lot of times I will look at a chord like that and say that these three notes work against four different chords. I mentioned Gmaj9. A lot of times if the band plays Gmaj7, I'll just play a D triad up the neck—or maybe two notes—and it sounds cool:

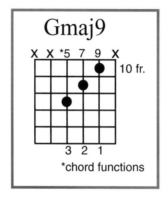

I kind of put that technique into everything. I'll break a chord down even though it might not be in the key we're in. Let's look at a regular 9th chord—E9 at the 6th fret, the one everyone knows:

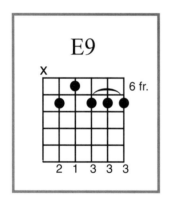

The other 9th voicing is this one:

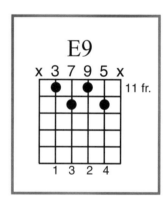

The difference is that here you have the 3rd of the chord on the bottom. Or you can leave it out:

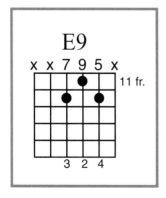

Now look at this G#m7♭5 chord—which is the same as an E9 chord with no root:

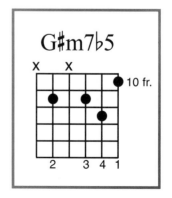

If I leave out the low G♯ and play the top three notes over an open E bass, it sounds great:

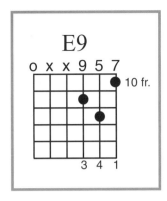

It's about choices?

Right. If I'm playing against an E9 chord, I could play G♯m7♭5 at the 11th fret:

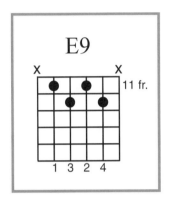

Or I can play it down at the 3rd fret:

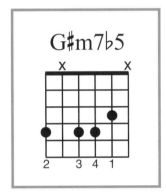

Or I can leave out the low G♯ of that chord and play a open low E instead:

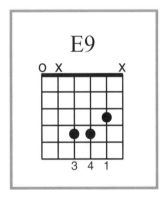

We've talked about taking a 9th chord and using the tritone—the 3rd and 7th of the chord:

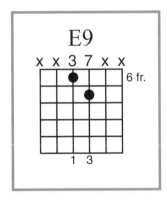

Sometimes I'll add the 9th of the chord to that, on the 2nd string:

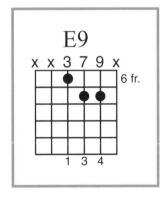

And sometimes I'll add the 5th of the chord to that, on the 1st string:

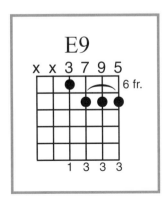

Or instead of the 5th, I might make it the 13th, two frets higher on the 1st string:

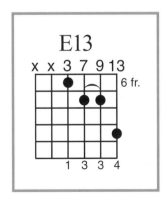

It becomes clear. If you break down chords, sometimes it just sounds so right. You can do that with all chords. The major 7th chord works well. Look at Gmaj7:

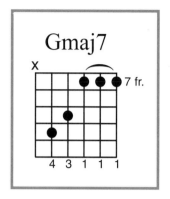

On the top four strings, you've got Bm7 there:

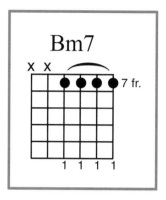

Also, if I'm playing off a Gmaj7 chord, I can play just two notes:

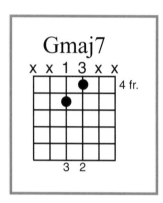

Or three notes:

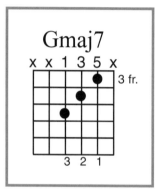

Or four notes:

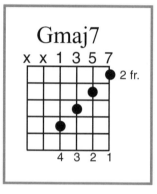

Here are some two- and three-note maj7 and maj9 voicings:

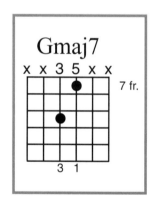

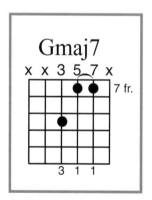

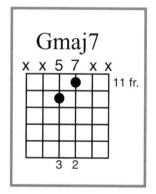

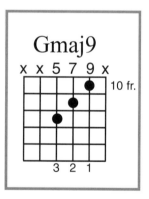

The maj7 and maj9 are pretty chords that you hear in the Motown sound. Take a Gmaj7 and make a pattern out of the voicings above. It's very simple. Less is more. I kind of came upon this on my own, but it's very simple. You double and triple your chord possibilities this way and you give yourself more options. Being a good funk guitar player is to be very instinctive.

Can you sum up what it's like playing in a good rhythm section?

Playing rhythm means being able to play with other people and being able to hang with other people. It's making relationships with people. It's about not coming off that I'm more important than you. We are all one rhythm section. Yes, I am a guitar player, Dave is a drummer, Rocco is a bass player, but we are a section. The reason why we sound good is because we work well together—we listen to each other. That comes from playing in bands and slugging it out in the garage. It's finding that common thread that comes from playing in a band. I don't think you can do that by reading a book. It's like being a golfer. You can read every golf book in the world, but you're going to slice into the woods unless you get out and play and hit the balls. It's batting practice or shooting free throws. It's very much like sports. A basketball team with five guys who all want to shoot the ball isn't going to win. Somebody is pissed off because they didn't get enough shots…didn't get enough solos. Somebody is overstepping their parts. That's the stuff that you slug out in the garage. If you find guys who are thinking the same, you've got a winner.

CREDIT

TRACK 14
Full Band

TRACK 15
Play-Along

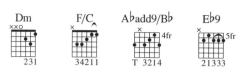

Words and Music by
Emilio Castillo, Stephen Kupka
and John Whitney

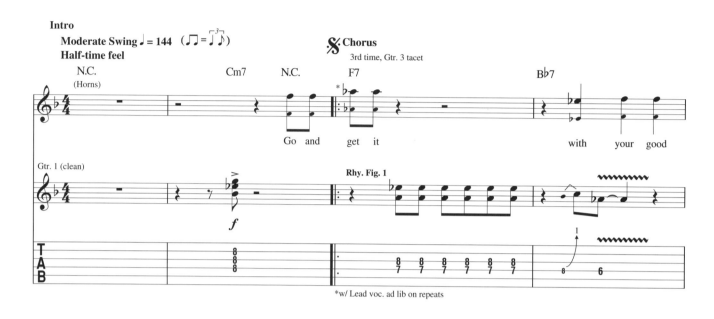

*w/ Lead voc. ad lib on repeats

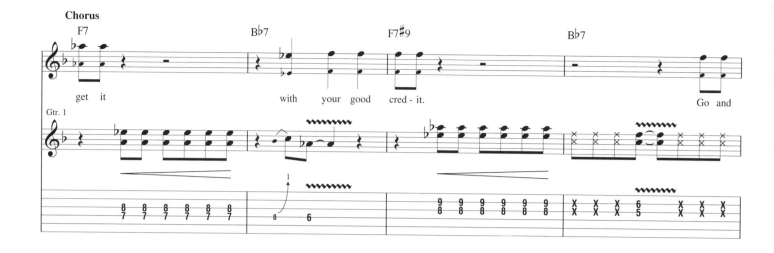

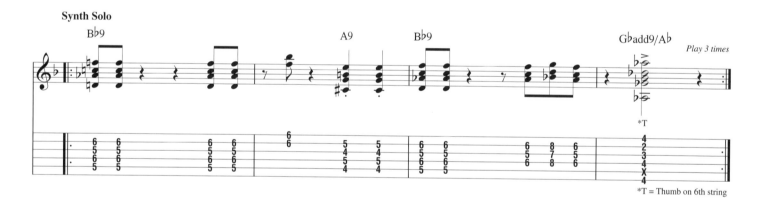

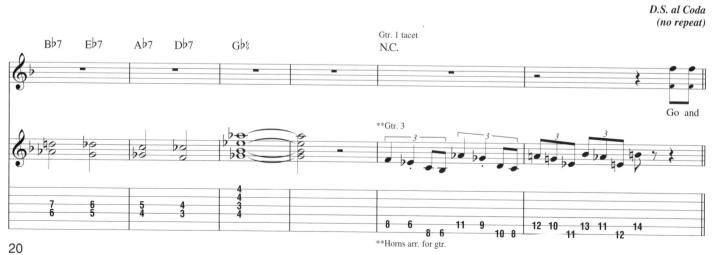

with your good cred-it. With your good cred-it. _____ Swing!

Outro-Chorus

w/ Lead Voc. ad lib

Go and get it   with your good cred-it.

2nd time, Gtr. 1: w/ Fill 2

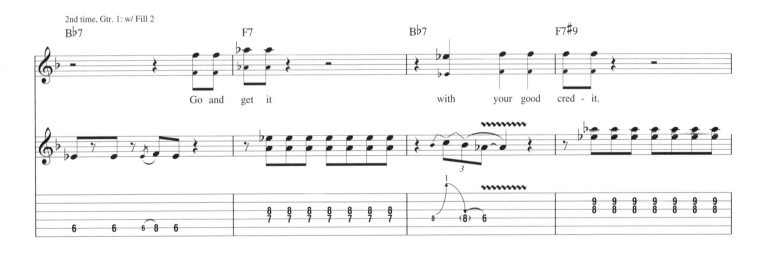

Go and get it   with your good cred-it.

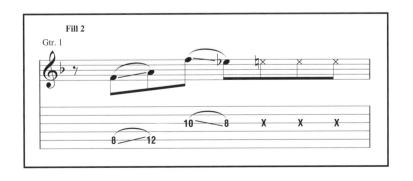

Fill 2

Gtr. 1

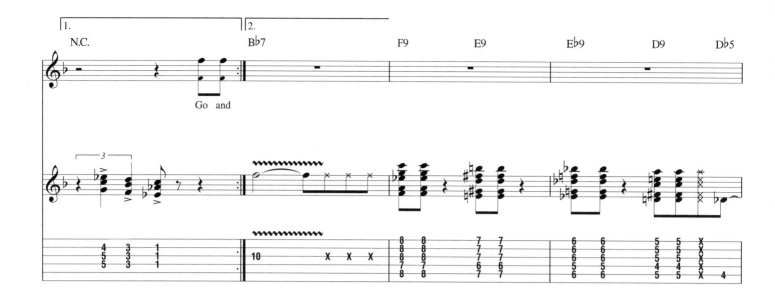

Go and

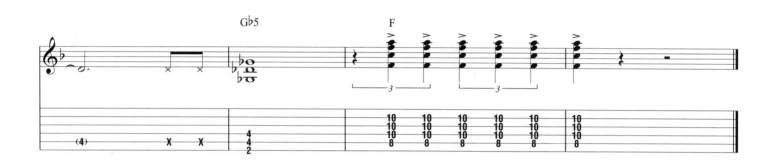

Additional Lyrics

2. You can pay your bills, cop a tailor-made suit.
   Sign on the line, you don't need no loot.
   Go and get it with your good credit.
   You can rent a car and fill the tank with gas,
   Cruise to the limit without no cash.
   Go and get it with your good credit. *(To Bridge)*

3. Impress your friends, do it to the max.
   And what do you know? You don't need no scratch.
   Go and get it with your good credit.
   Burn your ribs like ya done a lot of talking.
   That need a second look, and take a honey suckle, mother ain't no fool.
   Go and get it with your good credit. *(To Bridge)*

DOWN TO THE NIGHTCLUB

TRACK 16 Full Band TRACK 17 Play-Along

Words and Music by
Stephen Kupka, Emilio Castillo
and David Garibaldi

Intro
Fast ♩ = 208

(Drums)

Gtr. 1 (slight dist.)

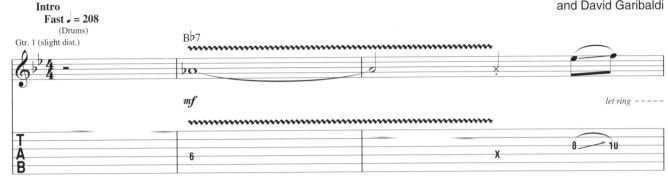

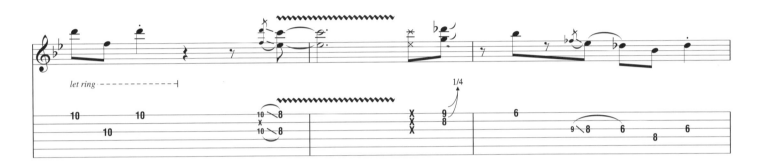

1. It's

Verse

Bb9

Sat - ur - day night, — I'm just hang - ing out, look - ing for a place to par-

2.,3. *See additional lyrics*

w/ clean tone

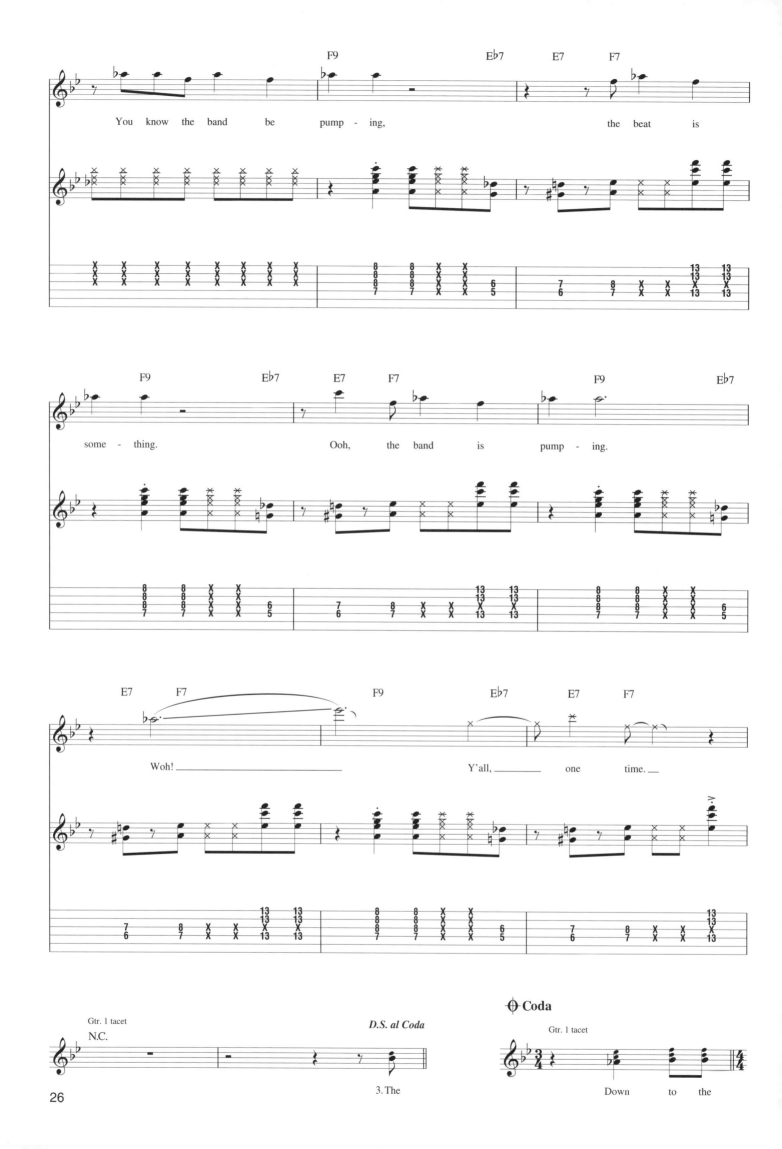

Additional Lyrics

2. Sitting by the dance floor, checking it out,
   Watching the man with the fast feet.
   He's got the hippest threads and the bad bugaloo,
   And a big old bag of tricks.

   2nd Chorus:
   Down to the nightclub.
   You can get what you want if you know where to find it.
   To the nightclub,
   We be slick, slick, slick. *(To Bridge)*

3. The night's almost gone and we're still going strong;
   The party's been so hearty.
   I hope it doesn't show while I'm driving down the road
   That I had too much to drink.

   3rd Chorus:
   Down to the nightclub.
   If you got the dough the liquor will flow.
   To the nightclub,
   Tied on a drunk, drunk, drunk. *(To Coda)*

THERE'S ONLY SO MUCH OIL IN THE GROUND

Words and Music by
Stephen Kupka and Emilio Castillo

Verse

Gtr. 1: w/ Rhy. Fig. 1

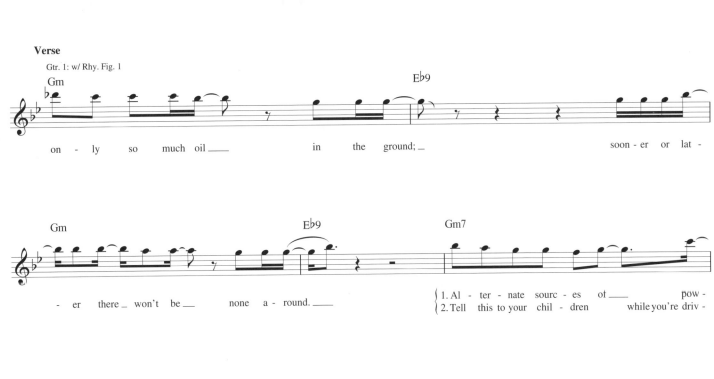

on - ly so much oil ___ in the ground; ___ soon - er or lat -

- er there ___ won't be ___ none a - round. ___

{ 1. Al - ter - nate sourc - es of ___ pow -
{ 2. Tell this to your chil - dren while you're driv -

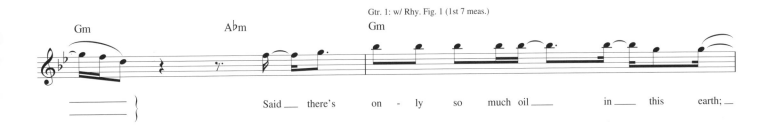

- er must ___ be found, ___ 'cause there's on - ly so much oil ___ in the ground. ___
- ing 'round ___ down - town, ___ that there's on - ly so much oil ___ in the ground. ___

Gtr. 1: w/ Rhy. Fig. 1 (1st 7 meas.)

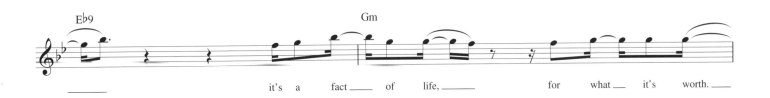

Said ___ there's on - ly so much oil ___ in ___ this earth; ___

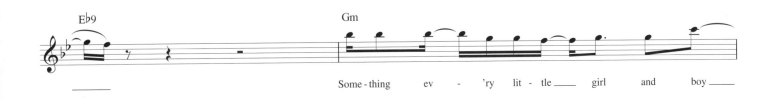

it's a fact ___ of life, ___ for what ___ it's worth. ___

Some - thing ev - 'ry lit - tle ___ girl and boy ___

___ should know ___ from birth, ___ that there's on - ly so much oil ___ in the earth. ___

32

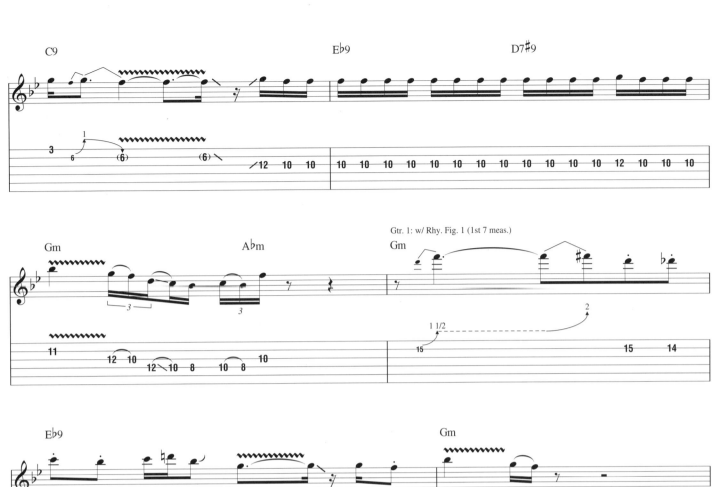

Gtr. 1: w/ Rhy. Fig. 1 (1st 7 meas.)

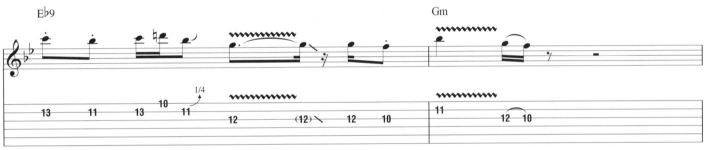

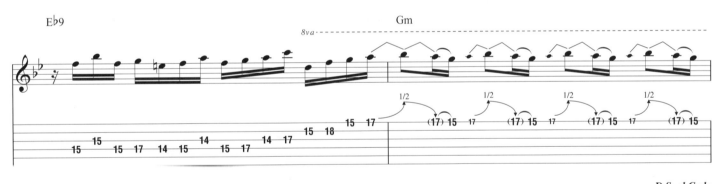

D.S. al Coda

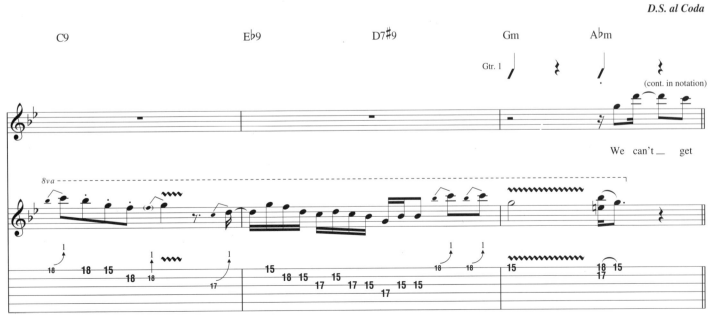

We can't __ get

WHAT IS HIP

Words and Music by
Stephen Kupka, Emilio Castillo
and David Garibaldi

Intro

Moderate Funk ♩ = 102

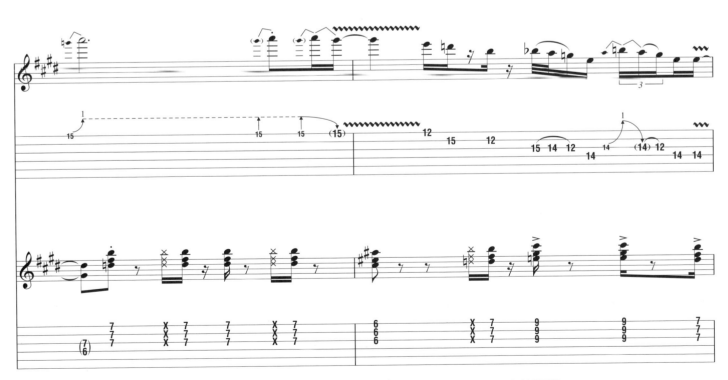

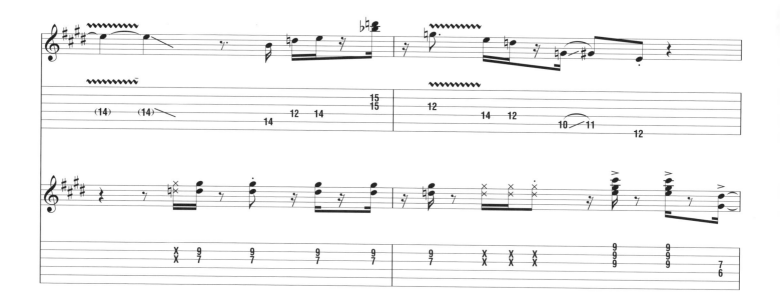

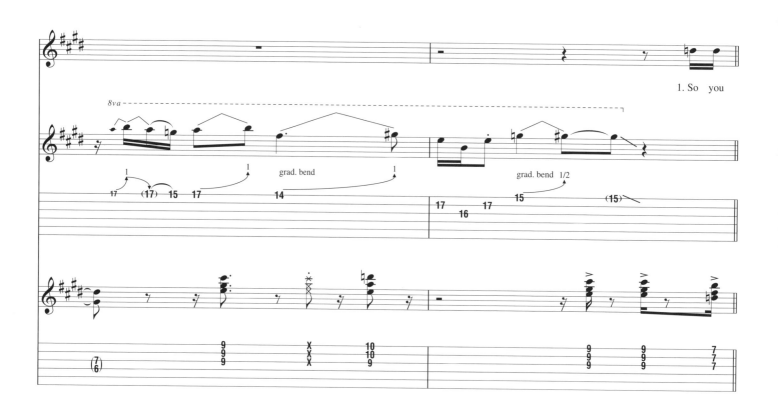

1. So you

Verse

Gtr. 2 tacet

E9

want to jump out __ your   trick __ bag   and ease on   in - to hip __ bag, __   but

2., 3. *See additional lyrics*

Gtr. 1

you ain't just __ ex - act - ly sure __ what's hip. __

Start - ing to let __ your hair __ grow, __ spend big bucks cop - ping a ward - robe, __ but

some - how you know there's much __ more to the trip. __ (What is hip? __

Chorus

E7#9   C9

Tell me, tell __ me, do you think __ you know? __ What is hip?) __

3. So you

Coda

Interlude

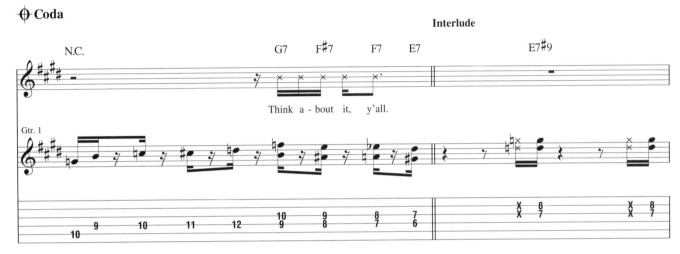

Think a-bout it, y'all.

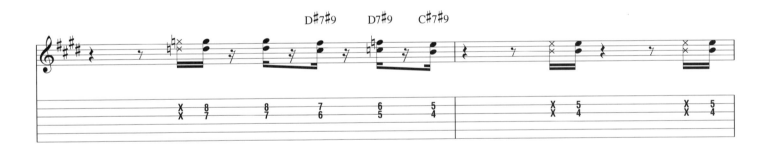

Outro

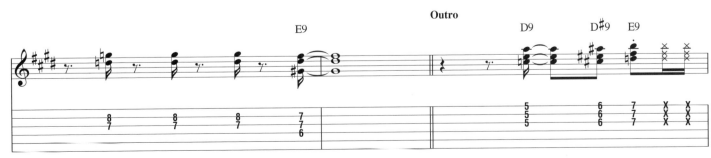

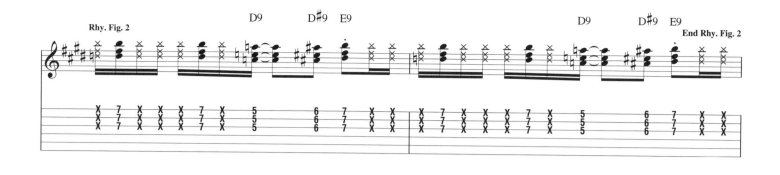

Rhy. Fig. 2 · D9 · D#9 · E9 · D9 · D#9 · E9 · End Rhy. Fig. 2

Gtr. 1: w/ Rhy. Fig. 2 (4 1/2 times)

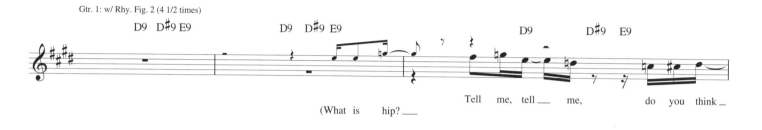

D9 D#9 E9 · D9 D#9 E9 · D9 · D#9 · E9

(What is hip? ___) Tell me, tell ___ me, do you think ___

D9 D#9 E9 · D9 · D#9 · E9

___ you know? ___ If you're real - ly hip, ___ the

What is hip? ___

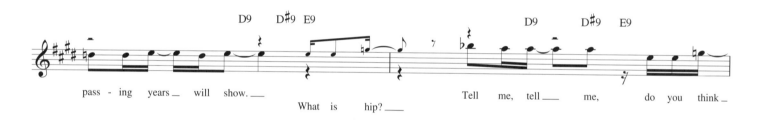

D9 D#9 E9 · D9 D#9 E9

pass - ing years ___ will show. ___ Tell me, tell ___ me, do you think ___

What is hip? ___

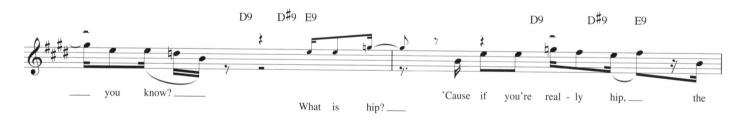

D9 D#9 E9 · D9 D#9 E9

___ you know? ___ 'Cause if you're real - ly hip, ___ the

What is hip? ___

E7 · E7sus4 · E9 · D9 · D#9 · E9

pass - ing years ___ will show, ___ y'all. Ah, ___

What is hip? ___

Gtr. 1

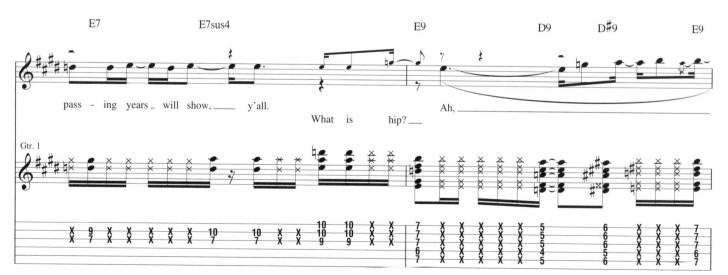

42

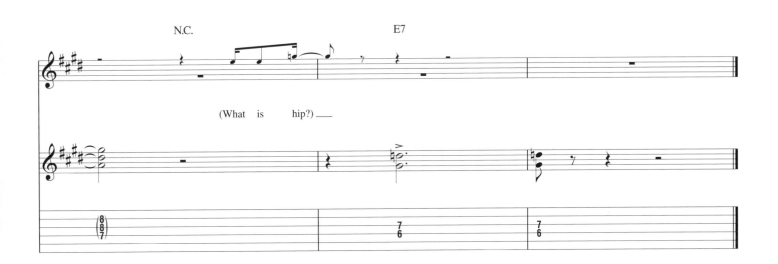

(What is hip?) —

Additional Lyrics

2. So you became a part of the new breed, smokin' only the best weed,
   Hangin' out on the so-called hippest set.
   Seen at all the right places, seen with just the right faces.
   You should be satisfied but still it ain't quite right. *(To Chorus)*

3. So you went and found you a guru in an effort to find you a new you,
   And maybe even managed to raise your conscious level.
   Now you're starting to find the right road; there's one thing you should know.
   What's hip today might become passé. *(To Chorus)*

DON'T KNOCK IT

Words and Music by
Francis Prestia, Jeff Tamelier,
David Garibaldi and Roger Smith

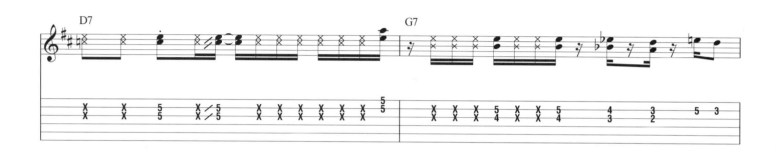

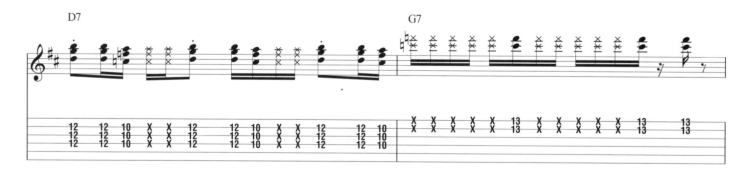

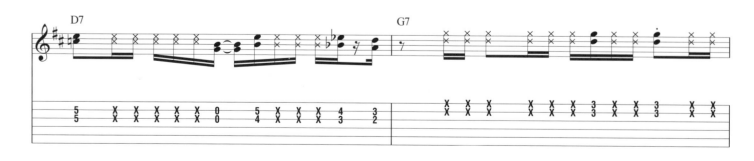

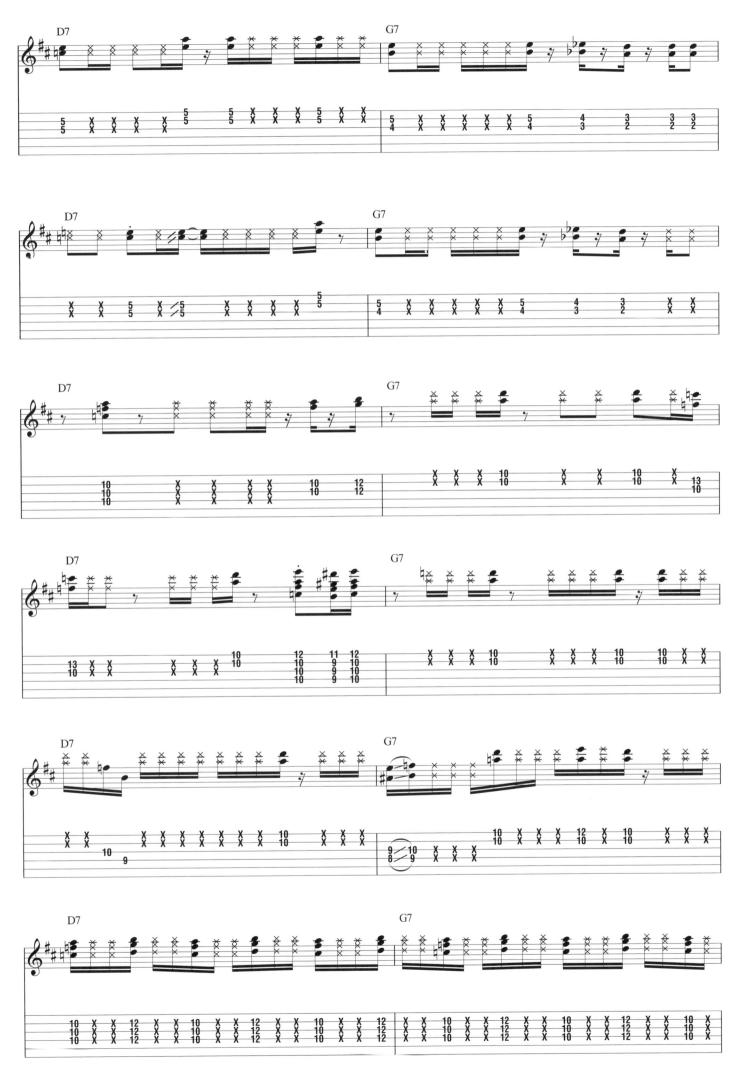

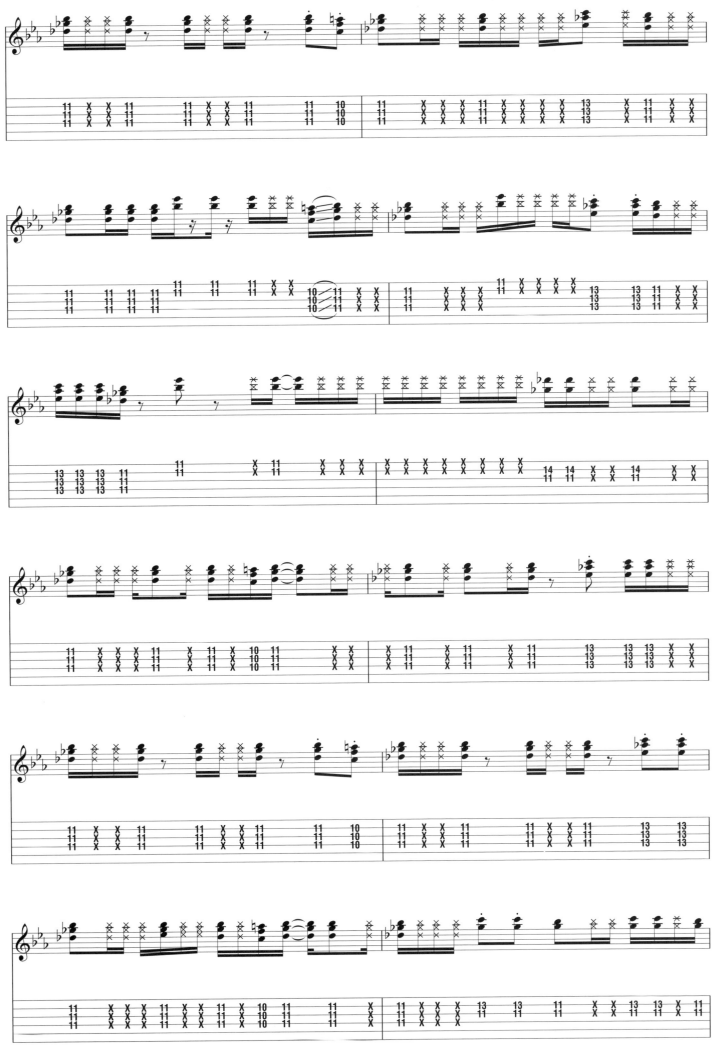

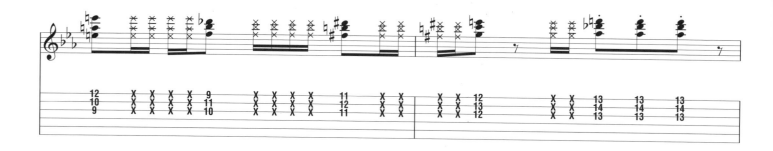

Begin fade

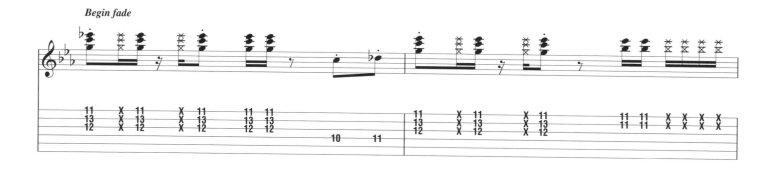

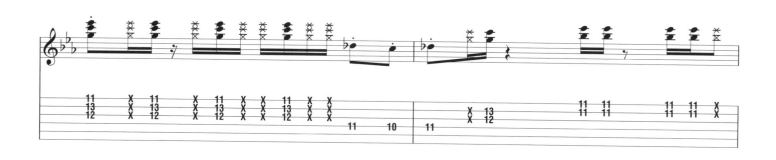

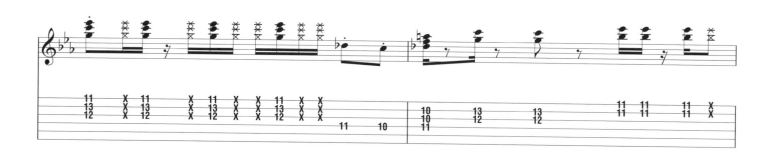

Fade out

F-FUNK

TRACK 24 Full Band
TRACK 25 Play-Along

Words and Music by
Francis Prestia, Jeff Tamelier,
David Garibaldi and Roger Smith

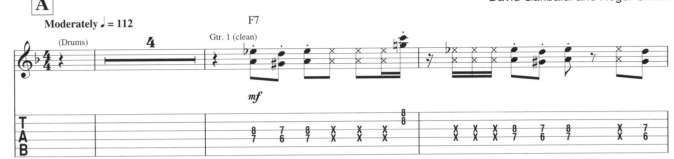

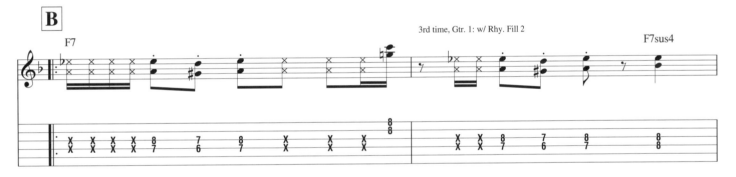

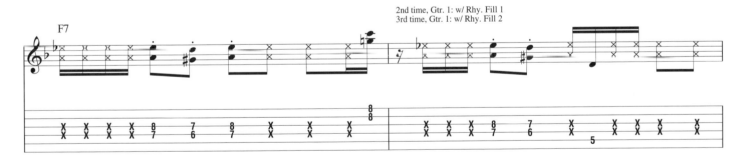

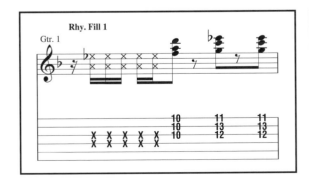

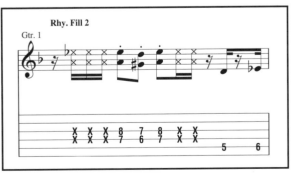

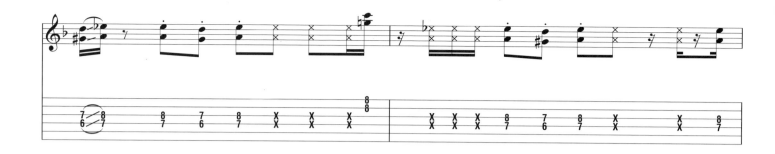

1.

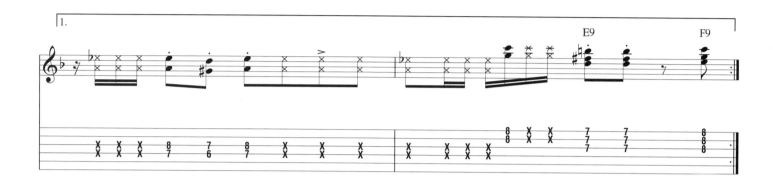

2.

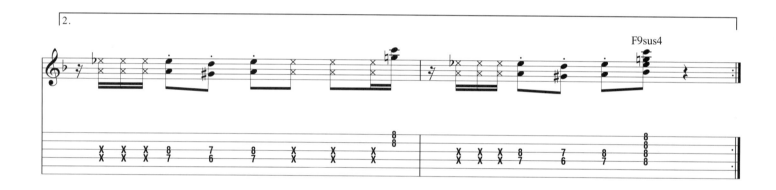

3.

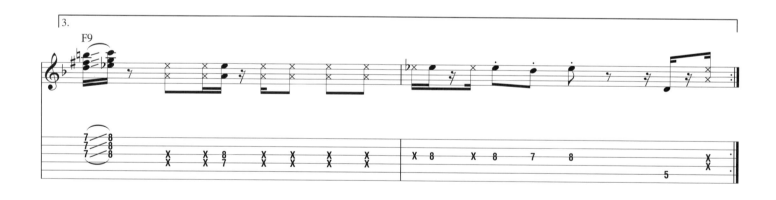

4.

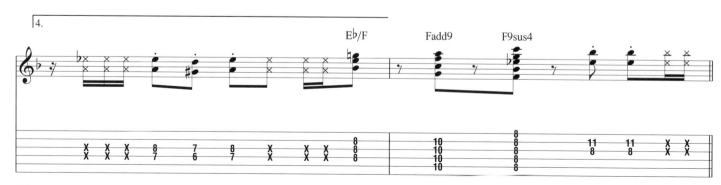

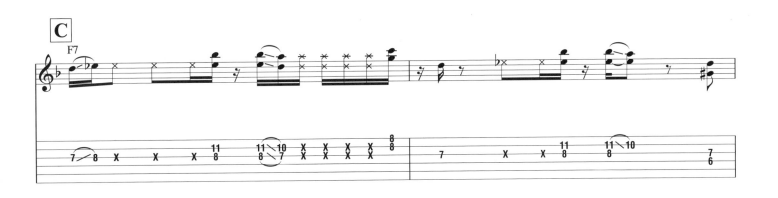

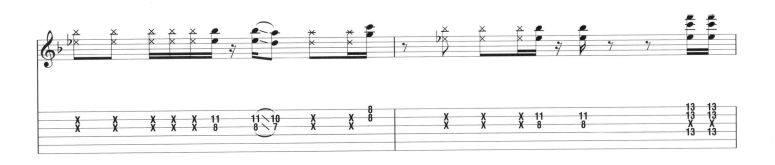

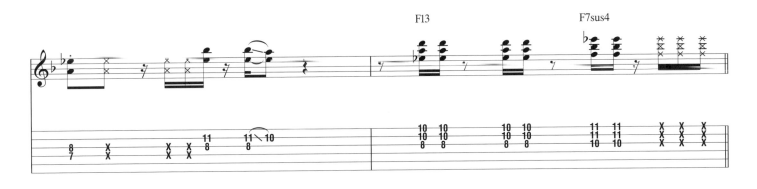

FREE FALLIN' FUNK

Words and Music by
Francis Prestia, Jeff Tamelier,
David Garibaldi and Roger Smith

HIP-E-JAM

Words and Music by
Francis Prestia, Jeff Tamelier,
David Garibaldi and Roger Smith

JEFF TAMELIER

In 1996, after touring for five years with '80s rock icon Starship (Jefferson Starship), Jeff Tamelier fulfilled a lifelong dream by joining the world-renowned soul band Tower of Power. Since then, Tamelier has toured the world six times with TOP, conducted workshops and massive clinics, and starred in the Hot Licks instructional video *Funk Guitar*. He has recorded four albums with Tower of Power, as well as his own solo effort, the critically acclaimed *Strat Got Yo' Tongue*.

When off the road, Tamelier is a prominent producer and studio musician in the San Francisco Bay area. He lives in Antioch, CA, with his wife, Debi, and his children, Jesse, Justin, and Samantha.

For more information, please visit www.bumpcity.com (click on "Updates," then on "Band Members," then on "Jeff Tamelier").

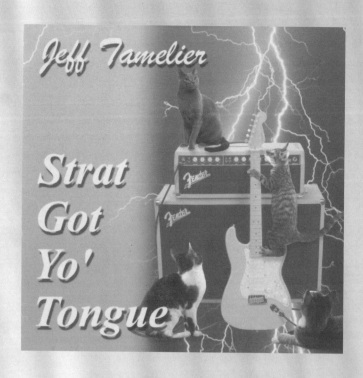